SKILLET
& SHEET
PAN
SUPPERS

D1307103

SKILLET
& SHEET
PAN
SUPPERS

FOOLPROOF MEALS, COOKED
AND SERVED IN ONE PAN

MONICA SWEENEY

THE COUNTRYMAN PRESS

A DIVISION OF W. W. NORTON & COMPANY

INDEPENDENT PUBLISHERS SINCE 1923

Photo Credits

All photos by Allan Penn unless otherwise noted below:

Page 8: © AlexeyBorodin/iStockphoto.com; 11: © LOVE_LIFE/iStockphoto.com; 12, 13, 22: © tbrainina/iStockphoto.com; 14, 17, 109: © Lauri Patterson/iStockphoto.com; 18, 87: © Brent Hofacker/Shutterstock.com; 21: © Maxsol/Shutterstock.com; 25: © ElenaGaak/Shutterstock.com; 27, 63: © martinturzak/iStockphoto.com; 42, 43: © AS Food studio/Shutterstock.com; 45: © teleginatania/Shutterstock.com; 47, 99: © Alena Haurylik/Shutterstock.com; 48: © Marina Onokhina/Shutterstock.com; 51: © Kiian Oksana/Shutterstock.com; 52: © thefood-photographer/Shutterstock.com; 55: © Anna Shepulova/Shutterstock.com; 56: © Katslaryna Belaya/iStockphoto.com; 59: © Piotr Krzeslak/iStockphoto.com; 60: © StephanieFrey/iStockphoto.com; 64: © papkin/iStockphoto.com; 78, 79: © Tatiana Brainina/Shutterstock.com 83: © Kati Molin/Shutterstock.com; 88, 91: © Liliya Kandrashevich/Shutterstock.com; 92: © robynmac/iStockphoto.com; 95: © iomis/Shutterstock.com; 96: © zi3000/Shutterstock.com; 100, 101: © alexandrshevchenko/iStockphoto.com; 105: © Yavgeniya Shal/Shutterstock.com; 113: adlifemarketing/iStockphoto.com; © 115: © -lvinst-/iStockphoto.com; 116: © Jim Bowie/Shutterstock.com; 119: © K2 PhotoStudio/Shutterstock.com; 120: © Kamila I Woojtek Cyganek/Shutterstock.com; 122: © GreenArt Photography/Shutterstock.com

Front cover: © minadezhda/iStockphoto.com; © Katslaryna Belaya/iStockphoto.com; © annal211/iStockphoto.com; © Debbi Smirnoff/iStockphoto.com; © Robyn Mackenzie/iStockphoto.com
Spine: Andrey Arkusha/Shutterstock.com
Back cover: © martinturzak/iStockphoto.com; © ElenaGaak/Shutterstock.com

For information about permission to reproduce selections from this book, write to Permissions, The Countryman Press, 500 Fifth Avenue, New York, NY 10110

For information about special discounts for bulk purchases, please contact W. W. Norton Special Sales at specialsales@wwnorton.com or 800-233-4830

Library of Congress Cataloging-in-Publication Data

Names: Sweeney, Monica, author.
Title: Skillet & sheet pan suppers : totally foolproof meals, cooked and
   served in one pan / Monica Sweeney.
Other titles: Skillet and sheet pan suppers
Description: New York, NY : Countryman Press, a division of W. W. Norton &
   Company, Independent Publishers Since 1923, [2016] | Includes index.
Identifiers: LCCN 2016017592 | ISBN 9781581574081 (pbk.)
Subjects: LCSH: Skillet cooking. | One-dish meals. | Dinners and dining. |
   LCGFT: Cookbooks.
Classification: LCC TX840.S55 S94 2016 | DDC 641.7/7—dc23 LC record available at https://lccn.loc.gov/2016017592

The Countryman Press
www.countrymanpress.com

A division of W. W. Norton & Company, Inc.,
500 Fifth Avenue, New York, NY 10110
www.wwnorton.com

10 9 8 7 6 5 4 3 2 1

TO ALLAN

SKILLET & SHEET PAN SUPPERS
CONTENTS

Introduction

There is something to be said for simplicity. While it's true that some of the best recipes take hours to slow cook and years to master, not every delicious arrangement of flavors has to be difficult. Better yet, it can be quick, inexpensive, and as easy as turning on the oven or lighting the stove. The recipes in this book celebrate two of the very best "one pot" cooking vessels: the sheet pan and the skillet. When pressure cookers and Dutch ovens get all the attention in the cooking community, the sheet pan and the skillet are the tried-and-true methods of cooking that will never disappoint.

On Sheet Pans

Sheet pans are the kitchen gods' gift to mankind. They're fuss free, particularly if you tend to line them with foil to avoid the pure torment of scrubbing off crusted-on grease and food. The sheet pans I refer to in this book are rimmed baking sheets. Flat cookie sheets without rims will lead to spills and mess in your oven, so you should avoid them. Some of the recipes will call for a "half sheet" or a "¾ sheet," which are fancy ways of saying small and medium sheet pans. If you have a half sheet but do not have the ¾ amongst your kitchenwares, fret not! Recipes like the "King-Size Calzones" can be cut in half so that you only make one, which will fit perfectly on the smaller of the two sheets.

While cooking on a sheet pan is one of the easiest methods you can master, it's not without its hiccups. Unless otherwise noted, food should be arranged in one layer on the sheet pan. This means that if you're tossing asparagus onto the sheet, they shouldn't be in piles or overlap. This will help ensure that your food is cooked evenly.

On Skillets

From stir-fries and pastas to frittatas and pizza, skillets are the everyman of cooking. The majority of the skillet recipes included in this book can be prepared in your run-of-the-mill large skillet, but there are a few in which the style of the skillet does matter. In the case of frittatas and pizza recipes, for example, you will need to use a cast-iron skillet. This style of skillet is perfect for meals that need to keep their shape and hold in heat, whereas risottos and chicken dishes can be prepared using your go-to large skillet.

Whether you're cooking for the whole family or are prepping your week's lunches, these pages offer a little something for everyone. Some of the recipes in this book require a little love and care, because no matter how easy it can be to make White Wine Shrimp Risotto, letting it sit without stirring for 20 minutes will have you in the market for a new skillet regardless. Other recipes, such as the Teriyaki Beef Stir Fry, require so little effort and taste so good that it feels like cheating. So whether you are well acquainted with sheet pans and skillets—and the miracles they perform—or you find yourself in the newbie crowd, this book has a whole range of tasty supper treats that will be on your plate in no time!

CHAPTER ONE

BEEF & PORK

Good Old-Fashioned Sausage Pizza

Deep-dish pizza cravings never have to go unanswered again with this quick and easy recipe. The beauty of this pizza is in the crust: the cast-iron skillet gives the dough the crunchy, flaky crisp that is nothing short of irresistible. With a little help from pre-packaged pizza dough and some classic ingredients, you can have a piping hot, crispy, and cheesy pizza in no time.

Yield: 4–6 slices

3 tablespoons olive oil, divided

1 (16-ounce) package pizza dough

1 (15-ounce) can tomato sauce

2 tablespoons tomato paste

3 tablespoons grated Parmesan cheese

¾ teaspoon dry oregano

½ teaspoon dry basil

⅛ teaspoon crushed red pepper

2–3 white mushrooms, sliced

½ green bell pepper, sliced

2 cups (8 ounces) shredded mozzarella

2–3 links (6–8 ounces) Italian sausage, cooked and sliced

Brush the inside of a 12-inch skillet with 2 tablespoons of olive oil. Transfer the cold dough directly from the bag into the skillet and let it rest, covered, for 1 to 2 hours.

Preheat the oven to 475°F. In a medium bowl, combine the tomato sauce, tomato paste, Parmesan, oregano, basil, and crushed red pepper, and set the mixture aside.

Gently press the dough toward the edges of the skillet, spreading the dough evenly. Brush the edges of the dough with 1 tablespoon of olive oil. Ladle in the pizza sauce evenly and then add the mushrooms and peppers. Sprinkle the pizza with mozzarella and top with the sausage. Place the skillet over medium-high heat for 2 to 3 minutes. Transfer the skillet to the oven and bake for 15 to 20 minutes, or until the sauce is bubbling and the crust is browned.

Breakfast for Dinner

Sometimes breakfast for dinner just hits the spot. This "kitchen sink" recipe of egg, potato, and bacon goodness is all held together with gooey cheddar cheese. The best part of this recipe is how forgiving it is; you can toss in whatever you have on hand for a mouthwatering breakfast buffet.

Yield: 4–6 servings

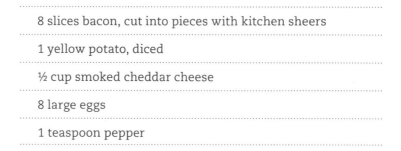

8 slices bacon, cut into pieces with kitchen sheers

1 yellow potato, diced

½ cup smoked cheddar cheese

8 large eggs

1 teaspoon pepper

In a large cast-iron skillet, cook the bacon for 1 to 2 minutes over medium-high heat. Pour out the fat drippings, add the potato, and cook for another 6 to 8 minutes or until the potato pieces have softened. Fold in the cheese. Crack the eggs over the mixture, cover, and let it cook for another 2 minutes or until the whites are no longer translucent. Sprinkle with pepper and serve from the skillet.

Cilantro-Lime
Beef Fajitas

Sizzling fajitas are in your future! This cilantro-lime marinade is nice and light, adding just the right amount of zip to these fiery fajitas. If you can't find cilantro-lime dressing in the grocery store, you can make your own by whisking equal parts lime juice and olive oil, a sprinkle of salt, pepper, sugar, and coriander, and a tablespoon of finely chopped cilantro.

Yield: 4 servings

1 cup cilantro-lime dressing (see headnote)

1 teaspoon chili powder

2 pounds skirt steak

1 large red bell pepper, sliced into strips

1 large yellow bell pepper, sliced into strips

½ medium red onion, cut into ½-inch slices

8 (6-inch) flour tortillas

1 ripe avocado, pitted and sliced for serving

1 lime, sliced into wedges for serving

Whisk the dressing and the chili powder together. Place the skirt steak in a large dish. Pour half of the dressing over the steak, coating it evenly. In a separate dish, coat the vegetables. Cover both dishes and let them marinate in the refrigerator for at least 1 hour and up to 6.

Drizzle a small amount of olive oil in a 12-inch cast-iron skillet and place it over medium-high heat. Add the marinated vegetables to the skillet and cook them for 2 to 3 minutes, or until they are browned but not overcooked. Remove the vegetables from the skillet and set them aside.

Using the same skillet, add a little bit of olive oil over high heat. Add the steak, cooking for 2 minutes on each side. Remove the steak and let it rest for a few minutes, then cut it into slices. Warm the tortillas for 10 seconds in the microwave and serve your fajitas with avocado and lime wedges.

Zesty Pork Fajitas

Enter pork fajitas with a zesty Italian flair! Save the time and stress of making a homemade marinade by grabbing a bottle of your favorite Italian vinaigrette salad dressing. These tasty fajitas will be sizzling on your stove in no time!

Yield: 4 servings

2 pounds pork tenderloin

1 cup zesty Italian dressing

1 large red bell pepper, sliced into strips

1 large yellow bell pepper, sliced into strips

1 medium red onion, cut into ½-inch slices

8 (12-inch) flour tortillas

Place the pork in a dish and coat it with the Italian dressing. Cover and refrigerate the pork to marinate for at least 1 hour and up to 6.

Drizzle a small amount of olive oil in a 12-inch cast-iron skillet and place it over medium-high heat. Add the vegetables to the skillet and cook them for 2 to 3 minutes, or until they are browned but not overcooked. Remove the vegetables from the skillet and set them aside.

Using the same skillet, add a little bit of olive oil over high heat. Add the pork, cooking for 4 minutes on each side. Remove the pork and let it rest for a few minutes, then cut it into slices. Warm the tortillas for 10 seconds in the microwave.

Apple-Sage Pork Tenderloin

Roasted pork tenderloin can seem intimidating to prepare, but it's actually super easy! All it requires is some easy-to-find spices and a little bit of kitchen twine to pull it all together for a delicious, beautiful looking meal. Just toss everything onto a sheet pan and you're minutes away from enjoying a sweet and savory feast.

Yield: 4 servings

1 pound pork tenderloin

1½ teaspoons sage, chopped

1½ teaspoons thyme, chopped

1 teaspoon garlic, minced

4 tablespoons extra-virgin olive oil, divided

5 bay leaves

3 teaspoons salt, divided

3 teaspoons pepper, divided

3 Yukon potatoes, chopped

2 large apples, sliced into wedges

Sprig of fresh thyme for garnish

Preheat the oven to 400°F. Grease a ¾ sheet pan with cooking spray or line it with aluminum foil. Slice the pork down the center, lengthwise, making sure not to slice all the way through. Pound the pork with a meat mallet to be about ¾ inch in thickness. In a small bowl, mix the sage, thyme, garlic, and 3 tablespoons of olive oil together. Brush the mixture onto the inside of the pork. Roll the pork up tightly and tie it off with kitchen twine, spacing the twine evenly a few inches apart. Season the outside of the pork with salt and pepper. Place 1 bay leaf on the pork for every piece of twine, then transfer the pork onto the sheet pan.

In a large bowl, toss the potatoes and the apples together with 1 table-spoon olive oil, 1 teaspoon salt, and 1 teaspoon pepper. Arrange the coated apples and potatoes around the pork on the sheet pan. Bake for 30 minutes or until the center of the pork reaches 145 to 160°F. Remove the sheet pan from the oven and let it rest for a few minutes before removing the twine and serving. Garnish with a sprig of fresh thyme.

Pancetta-Mushroom Risotto

Mushrooms and crunchy pancetta make this the comfort food of all risottos. The pancetta and the cheese add a perfect dose of saltiness, which means you will want to use low-sodium chicken broth so you don't overdo it. With cheesy Parmesan to bring it all together and a hint of aromatic turmeric, this tasty risotto will be a go-to for a filling, warming meal.

Yield: 4 servings

5 cups low-sodium chicken broth

½ cup dry white wine, divided

6 tablespoons butter, divided

4 cloves garlic, minced and divided

1 (4-ounce) package pancetta, diced

1 (10-ounce) package wild mushrooms, sliced

½ yellow onion, roughly chopped

1½ cups Arborio rice

1 teaspoon turmeric

1 teaspoon salt

1 teaspoon pepper

½ cup Parmesan cheese, shaved

½ cup arugula for garnish

In a medium pot, heat the chicken broth and ¼ cup white wine on low. In a 12-inch cast-iron skillet, heat 2 tablespoons butter on medium heat. Sauté half the garlic and all the pancetta for 3 minutes, or until the pancetta is crispy, and then remove the pancetta with a slotted spoon or tongs. Add the mushrooms and sauté for 3 to 4 minutes. Remove the mushrooms from the skillet and set them aside.

Melt 4 tablespoons butter in the skillet. Sauté the onion and the remaining garlic until the onion is translucent, about 3 minutes. Add the rice, turmeric, salt, and pepper and sauté for a minute or two. Stir in the rest of the white wine. Slowly ladle in about 2 cups of the chicken broth, bringing the contents to a boil. Reduce the heat to a simmer and allow the liquid to absorb. Continue adding the chicken broth about one cup at a time, stirring frequently and letting the liquid absorb before adding more (about 20 minutes). When the rice is al dente, stir in the mushrooms and pancetta and the reserved cooking liquid. Stir until everything is creamy, remove from the heat, and then fold in the Parmesan and top with arugula.

Sweet Rosemary Pork

Rosemary pork sounds like the makings of a wistful Sunday dinner that takes the whole day to prepare. With this recipe, the most labor-intensive step is peeling the apples—and that's not even necessary! The sweetness of the honey, apples, and squash with the savory rosemary flavor of the pork makes for an abundance of satisfying flavor. Be careful not to leave the pork in for too long so as not to toughen the meat.

Yield: 4 servings

½ teaspoon garlic powder

1½ teaspoons dry rosemary

1 tablespoon honey

2 tablespoons olive oil

4 (7-ounce) boneless pork chops

2 cups frozen and cubed butternut squash

2 medium apples, skinned and cut into 8 slices

Salt and pepper to taste

Preheat the oven to 380°F. Grease a ¾ sheet pan with cooking spray or line it with aluminum foil. Mix the garlic powder, rosemary, honey, and olive oil together. Coat the pork chops, squash, and apples with the marinade and arrange everything evenly on the sheet pan. Bake for 15 minutes, then broil on high for an additional 5 minutes, or until the pork is lightly browned. Finish with salt and pepper to taste.

King-Size Calzones

These enormous calzones look like they should be coming out of a fiery brick oven in Italy, but making them at home is so easy! Whether you use your grandmother's recipe for homemade meatballs or just grab a bag from the freezer section, these calzones are the doughy cocoons of a warming, hearty meal. Keep in mind that this recipe makes two king-size calzones to feed the whole family. For fewer eaters or smaller appetites, cut all ingredients by half.

Yield: 4-6 servings

2 (22-ounce) bags prepared pizza dough

2 cups jarred pizza sauce

1 (14-ounce) bag frozen meatballs, thawed and cooked

4 cups fresh baby spinach

2 cups broccoli florets

3 cups shredded mozzarella cheese

1 egg

1 tablespoon water

Preheat the oven to 400°F. Grease a ¾ sheet pan with cooking spray or line it with aluminum foil. Flour a flat surface and roll out the prepared pizza dough as you would for a medium pizza. Pour the sauce and arrange the toppings in the middle or on one side of the dough. Moisten the edges of the dough with water and then fold over to seal the calzone. Press the edges together with your fingers, or imprint with a fork. Whisk an egg and 1 tablespoon of water together to make an egg wash. Brush the egg wash over the calzone for a shiny, golden crust. Bake for 20 minutes.

Teriyaki Beef
Stir Fry

A tasty teriyaki that can be made in minutes, this recipe is poised for greatness at your dinner table. The secret to pleasing your palate is in the simple blend of sauces. If you aren't big on steak, simply swap it out for chicken or shrimp for a meal that combines rich flavor with oh-so-good-for-you vegetables and protein.

Yield: 4 servings

1½ cups teriyaki marinade

1 tablespoon soy sauce

½ teaspoon ground ginger

1½ pounds sirloin tips, cut into ½-inch slices

1 (16-ounce) bag frozen Asian-style vegetables

Preheat the oven to 385°F. Grease a ¾ sheet pan with cooking spray or line it with aluminum foil. Combine the teriyaki marinade, soy sauce, and ground ginger together. Toss the sauce, sirloin tips, and vegetables together and then arrange everything on the sheet pan. Bake for 15 minutes.

Italian Carnival Sausage

Found anywhere from county carnivals to great American ballparks, it's hard to resist the tempting aromas of spicy Italian sausage with peppers and onions. You can bring that nostalgia home with this simple recipe that needs little more than an appetite to prepare. Serve the combination alone or in bulky hot dog buns.

Yield: 4 servings

2 tablespoons olive oil
¼ teaspoon garlic powder
½ teaspoon dry oregano
½ teaspoon dry basil
1½ pounds Italian sausage
1 medium red pepper, sliced
1 medium green pepper, sliced
1 medium onion, sliced
Salt and pepper to taste

Preheat the oven to 385°F. Grease a ¾ sheet pan with cooking spray or line it with aluminum foil. Mix the olive oil, garlic powder, oregano, and basil together. Split the mixture in half, tossing half with the sausage and half with the peppers and onions. Broil the sausage on high for 2 to 3 minutes or just browned. Return the heat to 385°F and add the peppers and onions to the sheet pan. Bake for 20 minutes.

Easy Cheesy
Pepperoni Pizza

Some classics need not be tampered with, and pepperoni pizza is one of them. Just roll out a ball of pizza dough, toss on your favorite pepperoni, and call it a day. For a flakier, buttery crust, consider using crescent roll dough—just lay the dough out on the sheet pan and press the seams together before adding the toppings. The result will be a homey, comforting pizza that makes dinner a no-fuss, tasty event.

Yield: 4–6 servings

1 (14-ounce) bag refrigerated pizza dough

1½ cups jarred pizza sauce

3 cups mozzarella, shredded

½ cup pepperoni, sliced

½ cup red onion, sliced

Preheat the oven to 400°F. Grease a ½ sheet pan with cooking spray or line it with aluminum foil. Lightly flour a clean surface, roll out the pizza dough, and then arrange it onto the sheet pan so that it meets the edges. Add the sauce on top of the dough, leaving about ½ inch along the perimeter for the crust. Sprinkle the mozzarella evenly over the dough and then add the pepperoni and red onion. Bake for 20 minutes.

Chorizo Jambalaya

Authentic Creole jambalaya and Spanish paella are iconic rice dishes that bow to the savory trinity of seafood, sausage, and spice. Instead of choosing between the two, this quick recipe uses spicy Spanish chorizo instead of Andouille sausage for a simple but tasty jambalaya that you can make on short notice. So while you may not be able to make the journey to the Louisiana bayou or the coast of Valencia for dinner, these incredible flavors can still be found right at home.

Yield: 4–6 servings

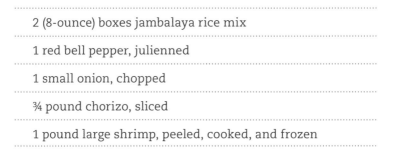

2 (8-ounce) boxes jambalaya rice mix

1 red bell pepper, julienned

1 small onion, chopped

¾ pound chorizo, sliced

1 pound large shrimp, peeled, cooked, and frozen

Preheat the oven to 400°F. Grease a ½ sheet pan with cooking spray or line it with aluminum foil. Spread the jambalaya rice across the sheet pan. Add the pepper and onion, and then drizzle water over everything (using the amount indicated by the rice mix instructions). Top everything with the chorizo and shrimp, and bake for 20 minutes. Reduce the heat to 350°F and continue baking for another 10 minutes.

BBQ Steak Tips

If you have six minutes, then you have time to make a perfectly cooked steak and crispy, crunchy asparagus. If you like your steak and vegetables to have a little char to them, keep them under the broiler for just a minute or two longer than the recipe calls for. With a quick dip in the barbecue sauce and a little flame, you'll have a juicy steak dinner on in no time.

Serves 4–6 servings

2 pounds sirloin steak tips

1 cup bottled barbecue sauce

1 pound asparagus

1 tablespoon olive oil

¼ teaspoon garlic powder

¼ teaspoon dry basil

Salt and pepper to taste

Marinate the sirloin in barbecue sauce for 1 hour. Grease a ¾ sheet pan with cooking spray or line it with aluminum foil. Preheat the broiler for 5 minutes. Fold aluminum foil into the shape of an open basket that's about half the size of the sheet pan. Place the asparagus inside the basket and sprinkle it with the olive oil, garlic powder, basil, salt, and pepper. Place the basket on one half of the sheet pan and the sirloin on the other. Broil on high for 1½ minutes, turn the basket, and then broil for another 1½ minutes. Remove the basket from the sheet pan, flip the sirloin over, and continue to broil the sirloin for another 3 minutes for medium-rare.

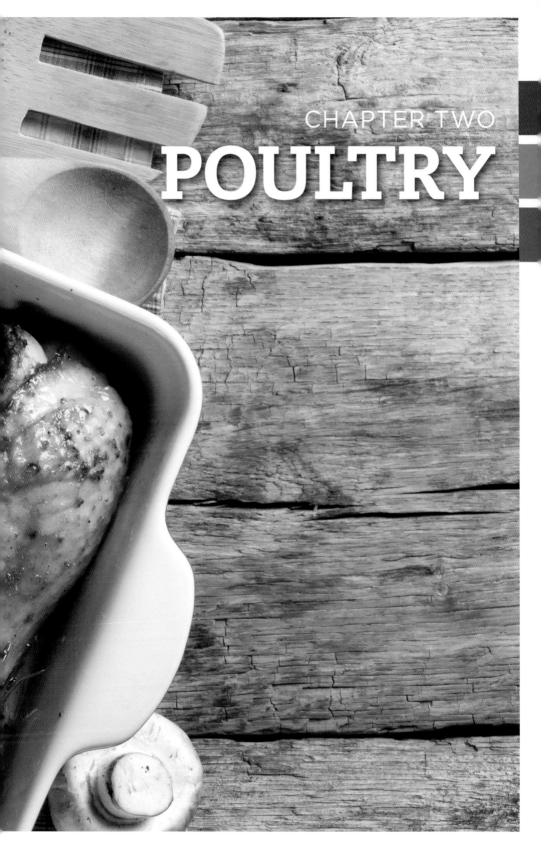

CHAPTER TWO

POULTRY

Tomato-Rosemary Chicken Braise

Paying homage to chicken cacciatore, this tempting blend of rosemary, mushrooms, peppers, and tomatoes is the perfect cloak of flavor for juicy bone-in chicken. You can serve this on its own, over pasta, or with a loaf of bread to soak up all of the tomato rosemary goodness.

Yield: 4 servings

8 pieces bone-in chicken

1 teaspoon salt

1 teaspoon pepper

½ cup all-purpose flour

2 tablespoons olive oil

½ red bell pepper, chopped

½ green bell pepper, chopped

1 cup chopped onion

2 teaspoons fresh rosemary, chopped

¼ teaspoon garlic powder

8 ounces sliced mushrooms

½ cup canned whole tomatoes, drained

1 cup marinara sauce

1 ounce Parmigiano-Reggiano cheese

Sprinkle the chicken pieces with salt and pepper, and then dredge them in the flour. In a large skillet, heat the olive oil over medium-high. Sauté the chicken pieces for about 5 minutes on each side so that they are browned. Remove the chicken from the skillet and set it aside. Reduce the heat to medium and add the peppers, onion, rosemary, and garlic powder. Sauté for 3 minutes and then add the mushrooms. Stir everything for another minute or two and add the canned tomatoes and the sauce. Return the chicken pieces to the skillet, ladling the sauce over them. Bring the sauce to a simmer over medium-low heat. Simmer for another 20 minutes or until the chicken is cooked through. Sprinkle with Parmigiano-Reggiano prior to serving.

Roasted Drumsticks & Veggie Medley

Crispy roasted chicken doesn't have to be a huge production. This skillet full of juicy chicken, healthy vegetables, and hearty potatoes makes for a well-rounded meal without too much preparation. You can certainly use fresh veggies while putting this dinner together, but prepackaged frozen medleys will cut down on the hassle while still keeping it tasting fresh and feeling wholesome.

Yield: 4 servings

8 pieces bone-in chicken

1 teaspoon salt

1 teaspoon pepper

4 tablespoons butter, divided

1 small red onion

4 Yukon potatoes, sliced

3 cloves garlic, finely chopped

Zest of 1 lemon

1 tablespoon lemon juice

2 cups frozen vegetable medley

Sprinkle the chicken pieces with salt and pepper. In a 12-inch cast-iron skillet, heat 2 tablespoons butter over medium-high heat. When the butter is foaming, sauté the chicken pieces for about 5 minutes on each side so that they are browned. Remove the chicken from the skillet and set it aside. Reduce the heat to medium and add the onions and the remaining butter, sautéing for 3 minutes or until the onion starts to look translucent. Mix in the potatoes, garlic, lemon zest, and lemon juice. Return the chicken pieces to the skillet. Simmer the mixture for 10 minutes and then add the vegetable medley. Continue cooking for 10 more minutes or until the chicken is cooked through, stirring the vegetables and turning the chicken occasionally.

Garlicky Chicken Wings

What this recipe lacks in fuss it makes up for in flavor—juicy whole tomatoes, plenty of garlic, and a hint of red wine vinegar turn this chicken into a delicious feast. Browning the chicken before you add the tomatoes and vinegar will make for a delicious, crispy skin that keeps the meat flavorful and moist.

Yield: 4 servings

8 pieces chicken wings

1 teaspoon salt

1 teaspoon pepper

2 tablespoons olive oil

3–4 cloves garlic, peeled

3 tablespoons red wine vinegar

1 (14-ounce) can whole peeled tomatoes, drained

1 bay leaf

1 teaspoon dry thyme

2 tablespoons butter

Sprinkle the chicken with the salt and pepper. In a large skillet, heat the olive oil over medium heat. Brown the chicken pieces for about 8 minutes on each side. Drain the fat from the skillet and then add the garlic. Stir briefly before adding the vinegar. Cook until the vinegar has mostly evaporated. Add the tomatoes, bay leaf, and thyme. Cover the skillet and let the mixture simmer for 10 minutes. Remove the cover and pull out the bay leaf with tongs. Reduce the liquid by about half and stir in the butter.

Classic Chicken Breast & Zucchini

A clean, healthy meal is only a few minutes away with this tasty chicken breast recipe. With a light dose of garlicky olive oil to add a hint of flavor that won't overwhelm, the chicken, potatoes, and zucchini will be full of flavor without being too heavy.

Yield: 4 servings

¼ teaspoon garlic powder

2 tablespoons olive oil

½ teaspoon dry oregano

1½ pounds chicken cutlets

2 large potatoes

2 medium zucchini

½ (10.5-ounce) container cherry tomatoes

Salt and pepper to taste

Preheat the oven to 385°F. Grease a ¾ sheet pan with cooking spray or line it with aluminum foil. Combine the garlic powder, olive oil, and oregano. Coat the chicken, potatoes, zucchini, and tomatoes with the mixture. Arrange everything on the sheet pan and bake for 20 minutes. Finish with salt and pepper to taste.

Winter Chicken Stew

This warming stew will be a welcomed relief from any wintry evening. If you have never made a roux before, the combination of flour and butter forms a smooth paste that helps thicken sauces. Be careful to wait until the roux is completely mixed and has lightly browned before adding the chicken stock, otherwise it will become gloppy. Make sure to have a fresh baguette or your favorite dinner rolls on hand, because the irresistible flavors of this stew are perfect for soaking up with bread!

Yield: 4 servings

8 pieces chicken drumsticks

3 tablespoons butter

3 tablespoons all-purpose flour

4 cups chicken stock

2 tablespoons tomato paste

1 clove garlic, minced

1 teaspoon thyme

4 medium red potatoes, peeled and sliced

2 carrots, peeled and sliced

1 cup frozen peas

Parsley for garnish

Preheat the oven to 300°F. In an oven-safe skillet, sear the drumsticks on medium-high heat until the outsides are lightly browned, about 1 to 2 minutes per side. Remove the chicken from the skillet and set it aside. In the same skillet on low heat, slowly incorporate equal parts butter and all-purpose flour (3 tablespoons of each). Mix them together to make a roux for 5 to 6 minutes until it is a light brown color. Gradually stir in the chicken stock and then add the tomato paste to thicken. Return the chicken to the skillet. Add the garlic, thyme, potatoes, carrots, and frozen peas. Transfer the skillet to the oven, covered, and let it cook for 45 minutes to an hour. Garnish with parsley.

Rosemary Chicken Kebabs

Lemon and rosemary make an excellent pair with these easy kebabs. The light dressing that can be made in no time is just enough flavor to bring these skewers to life, but simple enough that you don't have to go hunting for hard-to-find ingredients. While this recipe calls for peppers, zucchini, onion, and squash, you can feel free to add other ingredients like tomatoes, corn, eggplant, or whatever you happen to have on hand.

Yield: 4 servings

10 tablespoons olive oil

5 cloves garlic, minced

¼ cup rosemary

Juice of 3 lemons

1 teaspoon salt

1 teaspoon pepper

2 pounds boneless chicken

1 red bell pepper, sliced

1 medium zucchini, sliced

1 yellow squash, sliced

1 small red onion, sliced

Preheat the oven to 375°F. Soak 12 wooden kebab skewers in water while you prepare the other ingredients. Whisk together the olive oil, garlic, rosemary, lemon juice, salt, and pepper to make a marinade. Coat the chicken completely with the marinade and let it sit in the refrigerator, covered, for at least 1 hour. When your chicken is done marinating, skewer the chicken and the vegetables, leaving about ½ inch of space between each item. Grease a ¾ sheet pan with cooking spray or line it with aluminum foil. Place the skewers on the sheet and bake for 20 to 30 minutes, turning the skewers every 10 minutes.

Lemony Chicken Wings & Sweet Corn

This dish brings in the juiciness of roasted chicken and the simplicity of corn on the cob to make one fantastic meal, with tempting flavors that can be thrown together in a snap. You don't need to wait until corn is in season to make this quick and simple dinner.

Yield: 4 servings

1 pound chicken wings, separated at the joints and with the tips removed

¼ cup lemon juice

2 teaspoons garlic powder

1 teaspoon salt

1 teaspoon pepper

4 ears of corn, sliced into chunks (1 package mini corn on the cob)

1 (10.5-ounce) container cherry tomatoes

1 medium red onion, cut into chunks

2–3 scallion stalks, roughly chopped

Preheat the oven to 425°F. Grease a ¾ nonstick, rimmed sheet pan with cooking spray or line it with aluminum foil. Toss the wings in the lemon juice and then sprinkle them with the garlic powder, salt, and pepper. Arrange the chicken evenly across the sheet pan and bake for 20 minutes.

After 20 minutes, rotate the pan, flip the wings, and then carefully scatter the corn, tomatoes, and onion across the pan. (Separate onto two sheet pans if it becomes overcrowded.) Bake for another 20 minutes. Remove the pan from the oven and sprinkle the dish with scallions.

Rosemary-Mustard Turkey Breast

This hearty dinner of tangy mustard turkey and potatoes is a cinch. The recipe calls for frozen potato wedges, but you can also use freshly cut potatoes without adjusting the cook time. Just slather the turkey in this rosemary-infused mustard and pop everything in the oven for a succulent, stress-free meal.

Yield: 4 servings

3 tablespoons grain mustard

3 tablespoons Dijon mustard

¼ teaspoon garlic powder

2 tablespoons olive oil

1 tablespoon rosemary, diced

1½ pounds turkey cutlets

½ (32-ounce) bag frozen potato wedges

Salt and pepper to taste

Preheat the oven to 385°F. Grease a ¾ sheet pan with cooking spray or line it with aluminum foil. Combine the mustards, garlic powder, olive oil, and rosemary. Coat the turkey with the mixture, reserving some for later. Arrange the turkey and potato wedges on the sheet pan and bake for 20 minutes. Once it's finished cooking, sprinkle with salt and pepper and top with the reserved mustard marinade.

Skillet Coq Au Vin

The signature dish of the matriarch of French cuisine, Julia Child popularized coq au vin in the United States in the early 1960s, and it has remained a favorite ever since. A traditional recipe calls for Burgundy wine, but you can substitute with a dry red wine like chianti or cabernet.

Yield: 4 servings

4 slices bacon, roughly chopped

8 pieces bone-in chicken

1 teaspoon salt

1 teaspoon pepper

6 shallots, peeled and halved

8 ounces crimini mushrooms

¼ cup baby carrots

¼ teaspoon garlic powder

1½ cups dry red wine

1½ cups chicken broth, divided

4 teaspoons all-purpose flour

In an oven-safe skillet, sauté the bacon over medium-high heat until it's crispy. Remove the bacon with tongs and set it aside. Sprinkle the chicken with salt and pepper. Brown the chicken pieces in the skillet for about 8 minutes on each side. Add the shallots, mushrooms, and carrots, and sauté for about 3 to 4 minutes, or until they have browned. Stir in the garlic powder and carrots. Add the wine, 1¼ cups broth, and the bacon. Bring the mixture to a boil and let it cook for 10 to 12 minutes. Stir in the remaining broth until it's combined. Sprinkle in the flour, stir, and let your coq au vin thicken for 3 to 4 minutes.

Tarragon Chicken Thighs

Break out those garbanzo beans! Hearty chickpeas, earthy mushrooms, and a garlicky white wine sauce make this chicken dinner a nourishing affair. The crispy skin will be browned to perfection, absorbing all of the tasty flavors of the sauce.

Yield: 4 servings

2 tablespoons olive oil, divided

2 cloves garlic, minced

8 pieces bone-in chicken

1 (15-ounce) can chickpeas

1 (10-ounce) bag mushrooms

½ cup chicken stock

½ cup white wine

Heat 1 tablespoon olive oil in a large skillet over medium-high heat. Add the garlic, cooking for 30 seconds to a minute, or until it's aromatic. Working in batches, cook the chicken pieces for about 10 minutes, turning them over to brown each side. Remove the chicken from the skillet. Heat 1 tablespoon of olive oil in the skillet, then add the chickpeas and mushrooms. Pour in the stock and the white wine, stirring the liquids in with the other ingredients. Bring the liquids to a boil and then return the chicken to the skillet. Reduce the heat to medium and simmer for about 15 minutes or until the chicken is cooked through, rotating the pieces every five minutes or so.

Walnut-Ginger Chicken

Here's a recipe for some stir-fry chicken with a kick! This recipe's sauce is a blend of sweet and spice that makes for an irresistible yet easy-to-prepare, midweek meal. The combination of ginger and chili powder is great for spice lovers, but if you just want the zesty taste of ginger and the softness of honey without the added heat, simply omit the chili powder. The added crunch from the walnuts makes this stir-fry a fantastic balance of flavor and texture.

Yield: 4 servings

⅓ cup honey

½ cup soy sauce

2 tablespoons brown mustard

4 cloves garlic, minced

¼ cup ginger, grated

½ teaspoon chili powder

1 tablespoon olive oil

1 pound boneless, skinless chicken, diced

1 (10-ounce) bag frozen green beans

1 cup walnuts

Whisk together the honey, soy sauce, brown mustard, garlic, ginger, and chili powder. Pour half of the mixture over the chicken and let it marinate for at least 30 minutes. Heat the olive oil in a large skillet over medium-high heat. Add the chicken to the skillet and stir occasionally for 1 to 2 minutes. Once the outsides are cooked, reduce the heat to medium, add in the green beans, and then stir in the remaining marinade. Add the walnuts and cook for another 5 to 8 minutes.

Baked Italian Chicken

Get a delicious Italian chicken flavor with only a few short steps! The dry Italian seasoning packs on the flavor without having to sort through your spice rack. You can also substitute the dry seasoning with classic Italian dressing—just let the chicken and broccoli marinate in the dressing for 30 minutes before placing them in the oven. Hearty chicken and steamy broccoli make this a filling, healthy meal that will satisfy even the pickiest of eaters.

Yield: 4 servings

1 (16-ounce) bag frozen broccoli florets

2 pounds skinless chicken breasts, cut into 1½-inch pieces

1 packet dry Italian seasoning

Salt and pepper to taste

Preheat the oven to 380°F. In a large bowl, toss the broccoli florets, chicken breasts, and Italian seasoning together. Grease a ¾ sheet pan with cooking spray or line it with aluminum foil. Arrange the mixture onto the sheet pan in one layer and bake it for 30 minutes. Finish with salt and pepper to taste.

Creamy Garlic
Chicken

Cream of mushroom soup is the unsung hero of classic comfort foods, from beef stroganoff to green bean casserole. In this homey meal, the creamy soup cloaks the chicken and green beans in velvety, warming layers of flavor. What's more, the crispy onions top it off with an added crunch that brings everything together for the perfect cold-weather dinner.

Yield: 4 servings

1 (10.5-ounce) can cream of mushroom soup

2¼ pounds skinless chicken breast,
cut into 1½-inch pieces

1 (12-ounce) bag fresh green beans

10 cloves garlic, peeled

2 cups frozen pearl onions

¼ cup crispy onions to garnish

Salt and pepper to taste

Preheat the oven to 400°F. Grease a ¾ sheet pan with cooking spray or line it with aluminum foil. Pour the cream of mushroom soup into a large mixing bowl. Add the chicken, green beans, garlic, and pearl onions. Stir everything together and then pour the mixture onto the sheet pan evenly. Bake for 20 minutes, then sprinkle the top with crispy onions and broil on high for an additional 5 minutes, until the chicken has lightly browned. Finish with salt and pepper to taste.

Ranch-Style Baked Chicken

Transform ordinary carrots, potatoes, and drumsticks into an exceptional, flavor-packed dinner! While this trio is plenty enjoyable with just a little salt and pepper, the addition of dry ranch seasoning brings the combination to an irresistible level of flavor. A robust meal that takes a few short minutes to prepare, this crispy, mouthwatering arrangement will become a fast staple.

Yield: 4 servings

1 package dry ranch salad dressing mix

2 tablespoons olive oil

¼ teaspoon garlic powder

¼ teaspoon pepper

3 pounds skin-on chicken thighs and drumsticks

15 small yellow potatoes, halved

2 cups sliced carrots

Preheat the oven to 400°F. Grease a ¾ sheet pan with cooking spray or line it with aluminum foil. Mix the ranch dressing, olive oil, garlic powder, and pepper together. Toss the mixture with the chicken, potatoes, and carrots. Arrange everything on the sheet pan and bake for 30 minutes.

Lemon-Pepper
Turkey

There are few ingredients that can so reliably make a meal come together as lemon, and this easy recipe gives turkey and vegetables serious zest. Lemon-pepper seasoning can be found in the spice aisle, but for a quick homemade version, simply combine 2 parts lemon zest, 3 parts cracked pepper, and 1 part sea salt. With a little bit of lemon-pepper flavor, this nutritious, easy recipe can quickly become a dinnertime favorite.

Yield: 4 servings

1 teaspoon lemon-pepper seasoning

½ cup honey mustard

¼ teaspoon garlic powder

2 tablespoons olive oil

½ teaspoon dry oregano

1½ pounds turkey cutlets

1 pound asparagus

¾ pound Brussels sprouts

Salt and pepper to taste

Preheat the oven to 385°F. Grease a ¾ sheet pan with cooking spray or line it with aluminum foil. Combine the lemon-pepper seasoning, honey mustard, garlic powder, olive oil, and oregano. Coat the turkey, asparagus, and Brussels sprouts with the mixture. Arrange everything on the sheet pan and bake for 20 minutes. Finish with salt and pepper to taste.

Big Chicken Burrito

Nothing beats an authentic Mexican burrito, but these cheesy, spicy chicken pockets may be the next best thing! This recipe uses pre-cooked, pre-sliced chicken breast that can be found at the grocery store to make for a super fast, incredibly easy meal to put together.

Yield: 3–6 servings

1 (9-ounce) bag chicken breast, cooked and carved

½ (1.25-ounce) packet taco seasoning

1 (8-ounce) bottle taco sauce, divided

6 large flour tortillas

1 (16-ounce) can refried beans

1 medium red pepper, julienned

1 small onion, chopped

3 cups Mexican-cheese blend

Preheat the oven to 385°F. Grease a ¾ sheet pan with cooking spray or line it with aluminum foil. Coat the cooked chicken breast with the taco seasoning and 2 tablespoons of taco sauce. Lay the tortillas out on the pan and spoon $\frac{1}{6}$ of the can of refried beans onto each tortilla, making sure to leave an inch or two of space along the edges. Add even amounts ($\frac{1}{6}$ portions) of the chicken, pepper, onion, cheese, and taco sauce onto the center of the tortilla. Fold the right side over ¾ of the way across, fold the bottom lip up, fold the top lip down, and then roll the rest of the burrito onto itself to form a packet. Bake the burritos for 15 minutes, top them with sprinkled cheese, and bake them for another 5 minutes.

Cajun Wings & Rice

When you're too busy to carefully watch your stovetop rice, this sheet pan recipe saves the day. Perfectly cooked Cajun chicken and peppery rice that's tender underneath and a little bit crunchy on top make for an irresistible comfort-food feast. This arrangement calls for "dirty rice," but you can mix it up with wild grain or herbed rice selections as well.

Yield: 4–6 servings

2 pounds chicken wings

1 package dry chipotle pepper marinade

2 (8-ounce) boxes dirty rice mix

1 small red bell pepper, chopped

1 small onion, chopped

Preheat the oven to 400°F. Grease a ¾ sheet pan with cooking spray or line it with aluminum foil. Toss the chicken with the chipotle pepper marinade and let it sit for 30 minutes. Put the rice mix in the sheet pan and mix in the pepper and onion. Using the amount listed on the rice box instructions, pour 2 boxes worth of water over the rice. Lay the chicken wings on top of the rice. Bake for 15 minutes. Reduce the heat to 385°F and bake for another 25 minutes.

CHAPTER THREE
VEGGIES

Rustic Country Tart

Pie, pizza, gallete, or tart—call this cheesy, flaky meal what you will, but this is one dish that will have you going back for more. While you can certainly toss the toppings on in any old fashion you like, try arranging the potato, zucchini, and onion in an alternating fish-scale pattern. This will ensure that you get layers of each flavor in every bite!

Yield: 4–6 servings

2 sheets (one 14-ounce box) prepared piecrust

1 medium red onion, thinly sliced

1 medium zucchini, thinly sliced

2 medium potatoes, thinly sliced

2 tablespoons olive oil

½ teaspoon dry rosemary

½ teaspoon dry oregano

1 cup Gruyère cheese, shredded

Salt and pepper to taste

Preheat the oven to 385°F. Grease a ½ sheet pan with cooking spray or line it with aluminum foil. Lay the piecrusts out on the tray, allowing the extra crust to go over the sides of the pan. In a fish-scale style, overlap the onion, zucchini, and potatoes atop the piecrust. Drizzle the olive oil over the vegetables. Sprinkle everything with the rosemary, oregano, and shredded cheese. Fold the edges of the crust over to partially cover the tart. Bake, covered in foil, for 15 minutes. Remove the foil and continue to bake uncovered for another 15 minutes. Finish with salt and pepper to taste.

Mediterranean-Stuffed Peppers

There's no sense in using peppers as a vessel for ground beef when they're so much better served as nature's salad bowl. These peppers get all of the incredible flavors of a summertime pasta salad in the juicy packaging of a roasted bell pepper. You can swap out the orzo for rice or Israeli couscous if you so desire.

Yield: 4 servings

4 large red bell peppers, sliced down the middle and cleaned

2 tablespoons extra-virgin olive oil, plus more for drizzling

1 cup orzo

2 cloves garlic, minced

½ cup black olives, pitted

¾ cup canned chickpeas, drained and rinsed

1 cup loosely packed kale leaves, stems removed and chopped

⅔ cup feta cheese, crumbled

Juice and zest of 1 lemon

1 teaspoon basil, chopped

1 teaspoon red pepper flakes

¼ teaspoon salt

¼ teaspoon black pepper

Preheat the oven to 400°F. Grease a ¾ sheet pan with cooking spray or line it with aluminum foil. Place the bell peppers face up on the sheet pan and drizzle them with a bit of olive oil. Cook the peppers for 20 minutes, or until slightly browned. Cook the orzo in boiling water (with a dash of salt or olive oil) for 6 to 7 minutes, or until the pasta is al dente. In a large bowl, toss the 2 tablespoons of olive oil, garlic, black olives, and chickpeas. Add the cooked orzo and then toss everything with the kale, feta cheese, lemon juice and zest, basil, red pepper flakes, salt, and pepper. Fill the cooked peppers with the mixture and serve.

Healthy Hearty Breakfast Tarty

A quiche, a pizza, and a salad walk into a bar. . . . This sauceless egg pizza is a happy gathering of flavors that is filling without being too heavy. The flaky piecrust complements the cracked eggs, spinach, mushrooms, and peppers for a satisfying meal that is more fun than quiche and healthier than traditional pizza.

Yield: 4–6 servings

2 sheets (one 14-ounce box) prepared piecrust

2 cups baby spinach

¾ cup Swiss cheese, cut into ½-inch cubes

½ cup Gruyère cheese, shredded

½ cup mushrooms, sliced

½ cup red pepper, julienned

½ teaspoon dry oregano

½ teaspoon dry basil

8 large eggs

¼ cup Parmesan cheese, grated

Salt and pepper to taste

Preheat the oven to 400°F. Grease a ½ sheet pan with cooking spray or line it with aluminum foil. Place both crusts side by side onto the pan, working the dough into the pan with your fingers to cover the edges. Bake the crusts for 8 minutes and then remove them from the oven. Arrange the spinach over the crusts, followed by the cheeses. Add the mushrooms and the red pepper on top and then sprinkle with the oregano and basil. Crack the eggs directly over the pizza, being careful not to break the yolks. Sprinkle the Parmesan, salt, and pepper evenly over the pizza and bake for 20 minutes.

White Bean & Sundried Tomato Gnocchi

The potato that wants to be pasta, these tasty little dumplings are the perfect meal for a chilly day. With hearty white beans, healthy spinach, and zesty sundried tomatoes for a kick of flavor, this medley of ingredients is as tasty as it is nourishing.

Yield: 4 servings

1–2 tablespoons olive oil

1 (16-ounce) package gnocchi

¼ teaspoon salt

¼ teaspoon pepper

½ teaspoon red pepper flakes

1 (15-ounce) can white beans, drained and rinsed

¼ cup sundried tomatoes, diced

1 (10-ounce) bag baby spinach

¼ cup Parmesan cheese for sprinkling

Heat olive oil in a large skillet over medium-high heat. In the skillet, sprinkle the gnocchi with salt, pepper, and red pepper flakes. Cook the gnocchi, stirring occasionally, for 10 minutes or until the sides are slightly browned. Add the white beans, sundried tomatoes, and spinach to the skillet. Let the spinach wilt down, stirring occasionally, and cook everything until it's heated through. Sprinkle the dish with Parmesan cheese before serving.

Chili-Broccoli
Frittata

Frittatas and spice make everything nice! Fresh broccoli will always have the best flavor and consistency in a frittata, but you can also use frozen. Just make sure to defrost and pat the broccoli dry before adding it to your egg mixture. Fiery jalapeños add just the right kick to heat up this broccoli frittata.

Yield: 4 servings

2 tablespoons olive oil, divided

1 small red onion

2 cups broccoli florets

2 cloves garlic, minced

8 eggs

2 tablespoons milk

1 teaspoon salt

1 teaspoon pepper

1 jalapeño pepper, sliced

½ cup sharp cheddar cheese, grated

Heat 1 tablespoon of olive oil in a 12-inch skillet over medium-high heat. Cook the onion for 5 minutes. Add the broccoli and cook for another 2 minutes, making sure to stir frequently. Stir in the garlic, cooking for 30 seconds or until it becomes aromatic. Remove the broccoli from the heat. In a separate bowl, beat the eggs, milk, salt, and pepper together. Fold in the broccoli, jalapeño, and sharp cheddar.

Heat 1 tablespoon of olive oil in the skillet over medium heat. Once the skillet is hot, pour in the egg mixture evenly. During the first few minutes, use a spatula to lift the undersides of the frittata and to distribute more of the runny egg. Turn the heat to low, cover the skillet, and cook for 10 minutes. Check on the frittata during this time with a spatula, making sure the bottom layer doesn't burn. Once most of the egg is cooked (the top will still be a bit runny), transfer the skillet to the top rack of the oven to broil for 1 to 2 minutes or until the frittata is lightly browned. Let it cool for at least five minutes before serving.

Shakshouka

Shakshouka is a North African dish of eggs, tomato sauce, peppers, and spices. It's a popular breakfast in Israel and is best served with a fresh loaf of bread, pita, or challah for soaking up the delicious aromatic tomato sauce. The hearty poached eggs and peppery sauce make for a flawless, warming winter supper.

Yield: 4 servings

3 tablespoons canola oil

1 large yellow onion, chopped

½ red bell pepper, chopped

½ yellow bell pepper, chopped

1 jalapeño pepper, seeded and sliced

1 teaspoon garlic powder

¼ cup tomato paste

1 (28-ounce) can whole peeled tomatoes, crushed by hand

2½ tablespoons sugar

1½ tablespoons salt

1 tablespoon paprika

1 teaspoon ground cumin

1½ teaspoons freshly ground black pepper

8 large eggs

¼ cup scallions

In a large skillet, heat the oil over medium heat. Add in the onions. Sauté them for 5 to 10 minutes or until they are translucent. Stir in the bell and jalapeño peppers until they are softened, about 3 minutes. Add the garlic powder and tomato paste and stir for 1 to 2 minutes. Pour in the crushed tomatoes and then add the sugar, salt, paprika, cumin, and pepper, letting it simmer 20 minutes. Crack the eggs over the top and then cover the skillet and let it simmer for about 10 minutes, or until the eggs are cooked to your liking. Top with scallions and serve.

Cheesy Pea & Carrot Frittata

Quiche's low-maintenance sibling, the frittata, is all of the eggy, cheesy deliciousness without the hassle of piecrusts. If you prefer to throw all of your ingredients into one skillet and toss it in the oven in one fell swoop, consider microwaving the vegetables and the potatoes rather than sautéing them.

Yield: 4 servings

2 tablespoons olive oil, divided

3 medium russet potatoes, peeled and sliced

8 large eggs

1 clove garlic, crushed

1 teaspoon salt

1 teaspoon pepper

½ cup grated Parmesan cheese

2 cups frozen peas and carrots

Preheat the oven to 375°F. Heat 1 tablespoon of olive oil in a 10-inch cast-iron skillet over medium-high heat. Add the sliced potatoes and cook them for 6 to 8 minutes. Remove the potatoes from the pan and set them aside. In a medium bowl, beat the eggs, garlic, salt, and pepper together. Mix in the Parmesan.

Heat 1 tablespoon of olive oil in the skillet. Add the peas and carrots and cook them for about 2 minutes, or until they are defrosted but not overcooked. Add in the potatoes, spreading them evenly across the skillet. Pour in the egg mixture until the pan is evenly coated; reduce the heat to medium-low and cook about 2 to 3 minutes more, until the edges are set. Transfer the skillet to the oven and bake for another 15 to 20 minutes. Broil the frittata for the final minute for a golden-brown finish.

Tabouleh-Stuffed Eggplants

A little bit of sweet, a little bit of savory, and some hearty crunch make this recipe a flavor and texture delight. The pomegranate seeds give the whole mix some extra pep, but you can forego them if you prefer a savory-only dish. With the boxed tabouleh mix cutting down on prep time, you'll be on your way to delicious stuffed eggplants in no time.

Yield: 4 servings

2 medium eggplants

2 tablespoons olive oil

¼ teaspoon salt

¼ teaspoon pepper

1 (5.25-ounce) box tabouleh

¼ cup toasted pine nuts

¼ cup pomegranate seeds

½ lemon, zested and juiced

1 teaspoon parsley for garnish

Preheat the oven to 350°F. Slice the eggplants in half lengthwise and then score the insides without cutting through the skin. Drizzle with olive oil and sprinkle with salt and pepper. Grease a ¾ sheet pan with cooking spray or line it with aluminum foil. Place the eggplant halves face up on the sheet pan and cook for 40 minutes, or until slightly browned. Cook the tabouleh according to package instructions. In a large bowl, toss the pine nuts and pomegranate seeds into the tabouleh. Scoop the mixture into the eggplant bowls and top with lemon zest and juice. Garnish with parsley before serving.

Mushroom-Parmesan Frittata

Mushrooms make the meal in this classic recipe. A simple frittata that doesn't make a fuss, this combination of lightly browned egg, mixed mushrooms, and a touch of garlic and Parmesan make this egg creation a tried-and-true favorite. This recipe calls for a ¼ cup of Parmesan, but if you love your eggs cheesy, feel free to have a heavy hand and add more.

Yield: 4 servings

2 tablespoons olive oil, divided

1 (10-ounce) bag mixed mushrooms

2 cloves garlic, minced

8 eggs

2 tablespoons milk

1 teaspoon salt

1 teaspoon pepper

¼ cup Parmesan, grated

Heat 1 tablespoon of olive oil in a 12-inch skillet over medium-high heat. Add the mushrooms and cook for 3 to 5 minutes, making sure to stir frequently. Stir in the garlic, cooking for 30 seconds or until it becomes aromatic. Remove the mushrooms from the heat. In a separate bowl, beat the eggs, milk, salt, and pepper together. Fold in the mushrooms and Parmesan. Heat 1 tablespoon of olive oil in the skillet. Once the skillet is hot, pour in the egg mixture evenly. During the first few minutes, use a spatula to lift the undersides of the frittata and distribute more of the runny egg. Turn the heat to low, cover the skillet, and cook the frittata for 10 minutes. Check on the frittata during this time with a spatula, making sure the bottom layer doesn't burn. Once most of the egg is cooked (the top will still be a bit runny), transfer the skillet to the top rack of the oven to broil for 1 to 2 minutes or until the frittata is lightly browned. Remove the skillet from the oven, loosen the edges with a spatula, and let it cool for at least five minutes before serving.

Creamy Tortellini with Butternut Squash & Kale

The magic of tortellini is that it wraps the two major food groups—pasta and cheese—in one adorable little bow. While most pasta-lovers could eat tortellini plain and still be completely satisfied, this recipe adds a peppering of rosemary and a little bit of sweetness from the butternut squash for an even more incredible meal.

Yield: 4 servings

1 tablespoon olive oil

1 (12-ounce) bag cubed butternut squash

1 tablespoon rosemary

½ teaspoon kosher salt

¼ teaspoon freshly ground black pepper

1 cup vegetable broth

1 (5-ounce) bag kale, chopped and with the stems removed

½ cup half-and-half

1 (12-ounce) bag frozen tortellini

¼ cup Parmesan cheese for sprinkling

Heat the olive oil in a large skillet over medium-high heat. Stir in the butternut squash, rosemary, salt, and pepper. Cover the skillet and cook the mixture for 5 minutes, stirring occasionally. Pour in the vegetable broth and slowly add the kale until it wilts. Stir in the half-and-half, cover the skillet, and reduce the heat to medium. Bring the mixture to a simmer and then add the tortellini. Cook for another 10 to 15 minutes until the tortellini is cooked, stirring periodically. Sprinkle with Parmesan cheese before serving.

CHAPTER FOUR

SEAFOOD

Teriyaki Salmon

Salmon is the fish that can be dressed up in anything and still come out looking great. With a teriyaki marinade that can be whisked together in seconds, this is a tangy, savory meal that is packed with vitamins, protein, and hearty goodness. The sesame seeds add just a little bit of texture and flare to this easier-than-it-looks mealtime favorite.

Yield: 3–6 servings

1 cup teriyaki marinade

¼ teaspoon ground ginger

1 tablespoon soy sauce

6 (6-ounce) salmon fillets

1 medium red bell pepper, julienned

1 medium green bell pepper, julienned

2 cups broccoli florets

2 teaspoons sesame seeds for sprinkling

Preheat the oven to 385°F. Grease a ¾ sheet pan with cooking spray or line it with aluminum foil. Combine the teriyaki, ginger, and soy sauce together to create a marinade. Coat the salmon and vegetables with the marinade separately. Place the salmon fillets on the sheet pan, spaced evenly apart, and then arrange the vegetables around them. Bake the fillets for 15 minutes. Sprinkle with sesame seeds for garnish.

Lemon Haddock with Parmesan Asparagus

Panko-Parmesan asparagus may just rival French fries themselves. The crunchy and cheesy crust makes even the pickiest veggie-haters love a little green on their plates. The baked haddock pairs perfectly, and a little added lemon, salt, and pepper bring it all together.

Yield: 4 servings

4 (6-ounce) haddock fillets

Juice of ½ lemon

½ lemon, sliced

1 cup panko crumbs

½ cup Parmesan cheese, grated

1 teaspoon salt

1 teaspoon pepper

1 pound asparagus

½ cup all-purpose flour

2 eggs, beaten

Salt and pepper to taste

Preheat the oven to 400°F. Grease a ¾ sheet pan with cooking spray or line it with aluminum foil. Space the haddock fillets evenly on the sheet pan. Drizzle the fillets with the lemon juice and then arrange lemon slices on top of each fillet. Combine the panko crumbs, Parmesan cheese, salt, and pepper together. Dredge the asparagus in the flour, then the eggs, and then the panko-parmesan mixture. Arrange the coated asparagus around the haddock in a single layer and bake for 15 minutes. Finish with salt and pepper to taste.

Baked Caesar Salmon

If you ever top your Caesar salads with a fillet of salmon, then you know it's a match made in heaven. The garlicky, Parmesan flavor of the Caesar dressing lightly coats the fish and vegetables to add a tangy flair to this nourishing meal. If summer squash isn't in season, just trade it out for another vegetable, such as Brussels sprouts, asparagus, or carrots.

Yield: 4 servings

1 (1.2-ounce) package dry Caesar salad dressing mix

2 tablespoons olive oil

2 tablespoons lemon juice

4 (6-ounce) salmon fillets

1½ cups zucchini, halved and sliced

1 cup summer squash, halved and sliced

Salt and pepper to taste

Preheat the oven to 380°F. Grease a ½ sheet pan with cooking spray or line it with aluminum foil. Whisk the dressing, olive oil, and lemon juice together. Pour the mixture over the salmon fillets and space the fillets evenly on the tray. Toss the zucchini and summer squash with the remaining mixture. Bake for 17 minutes. Finish with salt and pepper to taste.

Kale & Pine Nut Cod

A light and healthy meal is easy to put together with this little assembly line of fresh ingredients. By placing all of the ingredients into serving-size pouches, the final result will be fish that's juicy and flavorful and veggies that are perfectly steamed. Add pine nuts for an additional crunch, and you have a perfect combination of textures.

Yield: 4 servings

2 cups kale leaves, roughly chopped

⅓ cup pine nuts

1 (10.5-ounce) container cherry tomatoes

4 (6-ounce) cod fillets

Juice of ½ lemon

4 teaspoons butter

4 sprigs fresh thyme

Salt and pepper to taste

Preheat the oven to 400°F. On four separate pieces of aluminum foil, create even piles of the kale, pine nuts, and cherry tomatoes. Lay one fish fillet on top of each pile and squeeze lemon juice over each. Place 1 teaspoon of butter on top of each, followed by a sprig of thyme. Fold up and close the foil around the bundles to create pockets and place them all on a ¾ sheet pan. Bake the fish for 20 minutes or until it is cooked through. Pierce the pouches to release steam before unfolding. Transfer the fillets to a plate using a slotted spoon and then season with salt and pepper to taste.

Toasted Sesame Shrimp

Shrimp lovers, unite! This recipe requires so little effort that you won't quite know how to go back to hovering over a stove. Buying pre-peeled raw shrimp means you'll minimize your prep time, so that all you have to do is toss everything together, throw it on a sheet pan, and—within minutes—an exceptional dinner will be on the table.

Yield: 4 servings

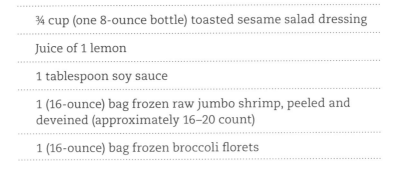

¾ cup (one 8-ounce bottle) toasted sesame salad dressing

Juice of 1 lemon

1 tablespoon soy sauce

1 (16-ounce) bag frozen raw jumbo shrimp, peeled and deveined (approximately 16–20 count)

1 (16-ounce) bag frozen broccoli florets

Preheat the oven to 400°F. Mix the salad dressing, lemon juice, and soy sauce together. Toss the shrimp and broccoli in the sauce until everything is coated evenly. Grease a ¾ sheet pan with cooking spray or line it with aluminum foil. Arrange the mixture onto the sheet pan in one layer. Bake for 30 minutes.

Fennel Artichoke Haddock

Hearty haddock with a Mediterranean flair, the combination of artichoke, olives, fennel, and a little bit of white wine infuse this meal with incredible flavor. For thicker pieces of fish, extend the cook time by another few minutes.

Yield: 4 servings

½ (14-ounce) can artichoke hearts, drained

½ (14-ounce) can pitted black olives, drained

½ bulb fennel, sliced

4 (6-ounce) haddock fillets

½ lemon

4 teaspoons butter

Splash of dry white wine

Salt and pepper to taste

Preheat the oven to 400°F. On four separate pieces of aluminum foil, create even piles of the artichoke hearts, olives, and fennel. Lay one fish fillet on top of each pile and squeeze lemon juice over each. Place 1 teaspoon of butter on top of each fillet, followed by a splash of white wine. Fold up and close the foil around the bundles to create pockets and place them all on a ¾ sheet pan. Bake the fish for 20 minutes or until it is cooked through. Pierce the pouches to release steam before unfolding. Transfer the fillets to a plate using a slotted spoon and then season with salt and pepper to taste.

White Wine Shrimp Risotto

Lemon, white wine, garlic, butter, and Parmesan—need I say more? Some risottos can be overly rich and heavy, but the zesty lemon and crisp white wine keep this lovely rice dish from weighing you down. This flavor combination makes for an endlessly satisfying risotto that warms you to the core.

Yield: 4 servings

5 cups chicken broth

½ cup dry white wine, divided

6 tablespoons butter, divided

4 cloves garlic, minced and divided

1 pound medium shrimp, peeled

½ yellow onion, roughly chopped

1½ cups Arborio rice

1 teaspoon salt

1 teaspoon pepper

Juice of 1 lemon

1 cup Parmesan cheese, grated

½ cup scallions, thinly sliced

In medium pot, heat the chicken broth and ¼ cup white wine and keep the heat on low. In a large skillet, heat 2 tablespoons of butter on medium heat. Sauté half the garlic and all of the shrimp for 3 minutes, or until the shrimp are just pink. Add ¼ cup white wine and let the mixture simmer for 2 minutes. Drain the shrimp and set both the shrimp and the cooking liquid aside for later.

Melt 4 tablespoons of butter in the skillet. Sauté the onion and the remaining garlic until the onion is translucent, about 3 minutes. Add the rice, salt, and pepper and sauté for a minute or two. Slowly ladle in about 2 cups of the chicken broth and the lemon juice, bringing the contents to a boil. Reduce the heat to a simmer and allow the liquid to absorb. Continue adding the chicken broth about one cup at a time, stirring frequently and letting the liquid absorb before adding more (about 20 minutes). When the rice is al dente, stir in the shrimp and the reserved cooking liquid. Stir until everything is creamy, remove the skillet from the heat, and then fold in the Parmesan and the scallions.

Sriracha
Crabcakes

Coastal summers are incomplete without the happy union of fish, spices, lemon juice, and breadcrumbs. Whether those come in the form of Rhode Island "Stuffies" or the time-honored Maryland crabcake, you can rarely go wrong. This recipe adds some extra spice to a summer favorite.

Yield: 4–6 servings

1 pound lump crabmeat

½ cup bell pepper, diced

2 green onions, chopped

1 large egg, lightly beaten

1 cup panko crumbs, plus additional for dredging

Juice of 1 lemon

2 tablespoons mayonnaise

1 tablespoon Sriracha

1 teaspoon Worcestershire sauce

1 teaspoon Old Bay seasoning

½ teaspoon kosher salt

In a large bowl, combine the crabmeat, bell pepper, and green onions together. Mix in the remaining ingredients until everything is evenly combined. Once blended, form small to medium patties from the mixture with your hands. Heat olive oil in a large skillet over medium-high heat. Sprinkle additional breadcrumbs over the patties and then place them in the skillet (working in batches, if necessary). Cook for 3 minutes on each side or until the patties have turned golden brown.

Lemony Salmon & Asparagus

A dinner this delicious shouldn't be so easy, but it is! If you like your vegetables cooked well, you can remove the salmon from the oven first while the rest cooks. Just be sure to put a tent of aluminum foil over the fish to keep it warm in the meantime. In just a few minutes, you and your family will be enjoying a hearty, healthy, and incredible meal!

Yield: 4 servings

1 bunch asparagus, trimmed

1 (10.5-ounce) container cherry tomatoes

2 tablespoons olive oil

2 teaspoons kosher salt, divided

1 teaspoon pepper

4 (6–8-ounce) skin-on salmon fillets

Juice of 1 lemon

Preheat the oven to 450°F. Grease a ¾ sheet pan with cooking spray or line it with aluminum foil. Using the sheet pan, toss the asparagus and tomatoes with olive oil. Sprinkle with 1 teaspoon of salt and ½ teaspoon of pepper, toss again, and then lay out the stalks and tomatoes evenly in one layer on the pan.

Place the salmon fillets over the vegetables, skin side down. Sprinkle with 1 teaspoon of salt and ½ teaspoon of pepper. Bake on the center rack of the oven for 10 minutes. Finish by spritzing everything with lemon juice.

Shrimp & Pesto Spaghetti Squash Bowls

Spaghetti squash is one of those magical gourds that can transform into something incredible in a flash. There's no need for fancy spiralizers or kitchen gadgets to turn this squash into a healthy pasta impersonator—you just need a fork, some mixed-in flavor, and an oven!

Yield: 4 servings

2 spaghetti squash

2 teaspoons olive oil, divided

6 tablespoons basil pesto

¼ teaspoon salt

¼ teaspoon pepper

2 jarred roasted red peppers, chopped

¼ cup Parmesan cheese, grated

12 cooked jumbo shrimp, peeled and deveined

Preheat the oven to 375°F. Grease a ¾ sheet pan with cooking spray or line it with aluminum foil. Carefully slice the squash in half, lengthwise, and scoop out the seeds. Brush the tops of each squash with 1 teaspoon olive oil. Place the halves face down on a ¾ sheet pan and bake for 45 minutes. Remove the pan from the oven and let the squash rest for 10 minutes. Using a fork, scrape the insides until the squash is shredded, being careful not to pierce through the skin.

Increase the oven temperature to 425° F. Scoop the spaghetti squash into a large bowl. Toss the squash with 1 teaspoon of olive oil, pesto, salt, and pepper. Fold in the roasted red peppers and Parmesan. Scoop the filling back into the squash bowls and top with the shrimp. Return the squash to the oven and cook for another 5 minutes.

Index